Each Time, a Forest

poems by

Carol Tiebout

Finishing Line Press
Georgetown, Kentucky

Each Time, a Forest

ACKNOWLEDGMENTS

I wish to gratefully thank and acknowledge the editors of the following
journals in which these poems were published in their original form:

Calyx: Night Sheep
New Ohio Review: In the Red Vinyl Booth of the Horseshoe Café
BoomerLitMag: Water and Straw
Poet's Corner, MyEdmonds: Full Weight

Publisher: Leah Huete de Maines
Editor: Christen Kincaid
Cover Art: Carol Tiebout
Author Photo: Susan Garret
Cover Design: Elizabeth Maines McCleavy

Order online: www.finishinglinepress.com
also available on amazon.com

Author inquiries and mail orders:
Finishing Line Press
PO Box 1626
Georgetown, Kentucky 40324
USA

Contents

Night Sheep

The two of us listened to them night after night from our bed, the fumbling on the stairs, the muddle of steps at the landing, the soft brush of wool against dark walls. The small flock that inhabited the night halls stayed to the open places. They didn't wander among the boxes that stood, long since packed, and waiting, stacked in corners and under windows, a miniature city rising up among the furniture. Those cardboard alleys and dish pack towers were the cat's terrain and she didn't so much as lift her head when they started up. For her, they were as common as soup cans. But we listened, listened from separate rooms. We never heard them from the same place at the same time. One of us would be at the desk, the other downstairs in the kitchen, one would be awake, the other would have just fallen asleep. It was only in the mornings when we compared notes that we put two and two together. One of the sheep had worn out saddle bags, another, a small blue flower pressed into the cleft of her front hoof. They should be crossing some alpine meadow, we thought, not these sheetrock canyons and carpeted paths. Then we would laugh, make jokes about leaving hay trails and buttered biscuits in a line out the back door so we could get some sleep, though when they left, we missed them, missed their steady hearts and the smell, the smell! Like everything we've ever lost.

Full Weight

The oxygen tanks have
disappeared. Caretakers gone,
I stand on my own leaning

against the kitchen counter like some dogs
have leaned against me, full weight
wanting to be met, watch the toast as it slides

off the rack, lands on the small blue
plate, feel the breath of my grandmothers,
mouths pulled back, lips blowing

warmth. Forever we have talked in the code
of dishes, spoon, lemon rinds, chanting
the delivery of herbs on tongue or meat to cell

walls. Now, in the center heart: this
leaf, this bowl, this crescent
moon hovering above the sink-
the weight both holding and gone.

Notes From the Purse of a Power of Attorney

There is this light that is my friend. She orders
pizza from her hospital bed where she waits
through gull gray days to be discharged, listens
to metal carts drum the hallways below the tin buzz
of fluorescent bulbs, watches the cold outside look
back at her through the window until a square
box clears the corner of her room and the smell
of tomato, sausage, and crust grin her tongue.

I spend my days on the phone with her doctors,
social workers, insurance company, PT, OT
and her always, always tired nurses
while sitting on my couch or walking the quiet
neighborhood slicked into raingear, peeling
lozenges from my pockets, waiting for the sky
to break and drop bolts through the trees.

On the days when I visit, gloved and gowned
in blue, she always asks for a cup of ice, puts
pats of butter from breakfast on top to keep
them in their squares.

After today's physician—the one who
slouches in the green plastic chair—delivers
today's guesses, a hint of Manhattan slung under
his vowels, I walk away, type notes

in my head that turn themselves
into songs my mother once sang. Outside
the double doors, I look down, count the steps
to the parking garage with its dark odors, lose
the melodies as I walk its slanted floors.

At night I dream of carnivals, contests
and spirit-born ceremonies that rattle
into clatter and costumes. Coins sing my pockets
and the dancing is always about to begin. Red, blue
and green clad contestants stagger into the ring
while the bells lift and clang into life.

In the Red Vinyl Booth of the Horseshoe Cafe

We traded Harvey Wallbangers, Velvet Hammers
and straight tequila, kicked Nixon and Agnew
around, came up with a board game about Camp David
that would use lacquered walnut shells and peas

as markers. When the acid slid in, clipping all the edges
in clear light, we fell out into the late-night street now
stuffed with one hundred thousand points of cool fog
that wrapped the curbs and thinned under the lamps

into a series of 3 foot worlds. A drunk appeared below
us, limbs curled up, waving like a crab that had been tossed
onto its back from its rocking bed to hard granite while still
holding the comfort of the sea. He looked up at me

with baby kissed blue eyes and asked, "Are you an angel?"
I thought for a moment maybe I was, maybe in the realm
of infinite possibilities, it could be there on certain
Tuesdays, my name in the index of Alan Watts' book under A.

Fifty years later the sky opens up and raindrops
the size of cats sing the hood of my car as it curves
past the turnoff to town. In a loud whoosh
deafening as a splash down, I no longer

understand why I would hold back any
from whatever walks into this minute
from the deep pockets of the world.

We'll Feast in Place

The winter sun is lifting with ice strength up from the roots
of its long deep sleep. The wind does a call back from the inlet
where the water is throwing white across the broken boughs
of its razed surface. The crows turn up, the first, as always,

to move in, to play with things as they are. It's hard
to be out here for long, seductive as the bright sun
is. Cold wind lifts the corner of the world but here
in this open stretch of grass above the Sound

there is the right kind of non-silence: tree, rustle, car, bird,
airplane, something fluttering. It keeps to the holding, to the quiet
I want to step into after being with this morning's storm-wracked
patient, away from his caregiver's shivering eyebrows, her eyes

below asking themselves and me a dozen times a minute: What
can I do? The suffering! The suffering! Away from how
they moved back and forth in daytime REM, looking through
the dreamscape kitchen with its pot of rice on the stove, the flowers

on the sill, looking for some sign when there was no chance
of seeing anything with those roaming, roaring eyes. Even when
they looked straight at me, they were under occupation-
a boat rowing back and forth between two impossible shores.

Let's roast the corn, braise some carrots, I would have
said if I could have reached them. We'll feast in place, walk
together into the back of this place, where even a moment

can petal open into eternity. To the already
crowded litany of dying, I'd have said,
There really is no such thing as crowding.

You Ask Me What I Get from Reading Poetry

I'll tell you—

How to make the night sounds become friends,
how to talk to strangers,
how a backward sentence can be exactly the same thing
      as a shaman twirling,
that you have to read things more than once, even
      if you don't have to.

How the sound of What can be like the slight puff
      of an owl's cheek just before it hoots,
that there are people in the world who are barking mad
      in a way that doesn't make you mad,
that you have to read things more than two times, even
      if you don't want to.

That we've pretty much always been this way.
That we wish we haven't been.
How to listen to strangers.
That sometimes, you only have to read things once.

How if you don't understand a poem
      you can ask it to meet you in your dreams,
how it may show up as a rude bear, a coffee cup or its stain
      or your eyes as they look at the stain.

Ears Filled with Soil

The walls in this house are thin, not like
those in the one we left, the one we loved
so much. Here, I turn under the sheets

and watch the movement
of my cells as they flip from front
to back, one here, one there, changing

the membrane surface from skin to fur, nail
to claw, then past that through carpet and wood,
through pipes and the long-buried stumps of elm

and oak. Scooping handfuls of dirt, I push
down to where sleeping bears come and bury
their dreams, their soft ears filled with soil. I wake

just before I reach them and so night after night return,
moving with singular effort, day-life fading behind
me. Except for one bright-bright afternoon frozen, full

of the lavender light of northern latitudes, each
person who passes squinting into the sun, skin
etched, pupils lost in glacier blue, burnt sienna, sea

green, each eye a galaxy alchemized from slivers
of light, peering from their folded lid nests
each one walking in front of, walking overhead.

Rain

falling, the rain she comes
falling, her home is a mystery we thought
we knew but in all the months she does not
come, the months when her wildfire sibling
snares-in, matchsticking the forests, she is away
      doing who knows what.
      We know then that we don't
      know, maybe we had at some point
      but the point is she has found a place
      away from us.   At times

we see her in the news tiles—running down slopes, lifting
streams, her arms glistening, ropy with new strength, glimpse
the terror she births on small screens in our dry homes.

When the ashed winds come, orange the air,
slide in under our doors and honeycomb
our lungs we forget what we saw, pray for her
return, remember only her grace.
We set up vigil, watch for her, catch
glimpses of her swirl out on the ocean,
coming near then lifting away, dancing upward
      into the blue cape of the earth
      while we stand parched thin
      until the cooling leans towards her
      and she at last consents to condense, lets the drops
      she's been holding in her cloud continents
            fall and fall and fall

Seizures Temporal

First, I felt the lifting,

no, before that
 an apricot pit
    fist size,
crevassed
and fossilized, inside
    the belly's heart signaled
 cave deep danger.
    Then the lifting, the taking flight
    from here to a place that is outside
 of place but still stands next to it.

Damage and thunder blessing, right and wrong the back
and front of each other, I shook for two days until I placed
a stone into the palm of my hand and felt it tendril in.
That was the day when my years became
    five and five, two sides of a cliff echoing me.
    The next day, new waves bloomed deeper in,
built high, broke far from shore, the lifting
and falling, a tongue now speaking, now silent.

            Months later, when I was tested, the nurse
            asked me to recite as many of the numbers
            she was about to speak as I could and I
            thought you'llneverbeabletodo that,
            bless you and bless so you do it
            different. A door opened and I watched as all ten
            numbers arrived, hung in the air in front of me like a
            gang of excited children elbowing each other.
            I said all of their names. A first, the nurse said,
            and I did not tell her it wasn't me.

The cab to Urgent Care slicked up smooth
to the curb. I saw long yellow hair swinging inside.
She drove in slow easy moves. When we got there, I asked
how much. She turned and said no charge
then smiled such a smile I knew she
was the light outside come in.

In the waiting room I listened
    to my friend's message, listened to her sing happy birthday
to me on my phone's tiny speakers, the wooden
arms of the chair holding me in place, the window
    behind it streaming sun, framing the mountain
range I could not see, though I could feel its ridges
    walk the bones of my back. I watched
the notes of the song go in
unfettered and her with it with no part
of me putting a hand up. Me seeing
all of that, all of what was gifted.

skin

this soft container
rounding my bones
cupping oceans and electricity
talking always talking
about temperature, pressure, threat
soft even at this age
making the me-ness visible
holding the earth and stone
ancestors and the salt-spark
of not-yet cells waiting
to open into the difference
between water and this thing I love
this life-thing that only moments
ago I wanted to shed so tired
I was of navigating the wild
outer surfs of living
that I forgot skin's loyalty
its perfect tenderness

We Sang You

We sang the elements of your ashed bones
back out into the world leaving
the quiet gray and cream-colored grains
to rest in place until spring.

Before that, we sang the spirit of you out
through the spider's web cradling the window
at the end of your room, its thin threads breathing
the winds of the storm that would make the morning
news. We sang you up and out into the quaking arms
of the night sky with our still seamed bodies.

Before that we drove
through our neighborhood, signal lights rocking
above the intersections, blinking red like mute klaxon
until we got to the highway where the power still
held, made our way along the empty roads
so we would reach you before the world woke up.

Before that, the phone ringing me awake, then
the soft-spoken Nigerian nurse reciting
what he found when he went to check on you.

Before that, I'd wondered what he would
say, how he would say it. Then I remembered
how you'd talked the day before about a film
crew that was in the hallway reporting
on a snowstorm that was, you said, blowing
and billowing out there. I remembered how you
stared at me, held my eyes in place, looked into
them to see if I believed you.

What I get From Reading Poetry

A word
pierces the pericardium
drawing sinew, hair-fine
behind it. Another word
enters and weaves
in and out,
in and out.
Another line ends
the stanza and a tear
in the fabric of me
is woven closed. I turn
the page and my eyes fall
down the slopes
of the world described
in heart language,
whale tongue
and berry juice.
My tissues alchemize
a portal, or is it
a door easing closed?
I once heard
that a wound is nothing
more than a change
we object to. Now
you sing this
into my blood
as it careens by.

Begin Again

The stars hang distant
from each other tonight, each

one a tiny brilliance
in the sparest of landscapes,

singing to each other in radiance
and flares through the millennia,

spinning in the unseen
fullness of dark matter.

Was it God's idea
to invite them to come closer?

To knit them into small whipping
tails that settled into one

embryonic thumbprint after another
that then cooled into vertebrae,

to try out a new language
as they then stacked

themselves one on top
of the other?

Does God chant: Begin
again, begin again, grinning?

Habitat

I try
to reconstitute what
a hug feels like

outside of my skin
pod of two plus
cat, how it might wrap

strange, how I might turn
back from it, run
behind my ribs, seek

out the sleek crimson
folds of my heart
where I could pace

its four soft rooms, watch
its doors open and
close in a circle.

Water and Straw

I'd been walking the floor of the ocean all night
mapping the terrain with the soles of my feet,
the current's direction as it moved through my hair.
At dawn I rose, the weight of me unearthly.

Mapping the terrain with the soles of my feet
I saw you standing in the orchard.
At dawn I rose, the weight of me unearthly.
Water poured from my ears, pooling on the hardwood floor.

I saw you standing in the orchard
a wheel of red apples circling you like a rising crown.
Water poured from my ears, pooling on the hardwood floor
as I made myself lift against gravity.

A wheel of red apples circled you like a slipped crown.
You were back in that place where you do not know who you are.
I made myself lift against gravity,
let the earth pull me into place.

You were back in that place where you do not know who you are.
I thought I should call you in to the house, to the room with its four
walls let the earth pull you into place
while the birds ladle their song into the morning.

thought I should call you into the house, to the room with the four
walls you knew inside and out, bend you into its container.
The birds ladled their song into the morning
as I walked myself forward towards the tasks of the day.

You knew it inside and out, bent yourself into its container
let it smooth your wilding eyes with its shielded windows.
I walked myself into the tasks of the day—
its square root rhythms, its amnesia about the morning star.

You let it smooth your wilding eyes with its shielded windows,
let the sun sifting its yellow through the curtains bring you home, walk
you into its square root rhythms, its amnesia about the morning star.
I left, drove a car, turned corners, purchased a straw broom.

You let the sun sifting its yellow through the curtains walk you home.
I heard chainsaws, barking dogs, smelled the undercurrents of damp
roots. I left, drove a car, turned corners, purchased a straw broom
and later, I swept the house clean.

Each Time, a Forest

The first time I saw her she said it was like lying
in the woods on a log with prickly leaves
poking her everywhere, everywhere. She
plucked at her shirt, at the covers, at the air. Nothing
I did helped—not straightening the blankets or offering
to massage her hands.

I was writing my notes, listening with one ear, noting
the smell of hand cleaner and spilled soup drifting beneath oxygen
lines and pink ironed sheets when I found a narrow path, one
that led to her. A simple question, saying her son's name,
or maybe that's just what it looked like.

The next time was better, I could walk right in. *Your hands, why
are they so warm?* she asked when I laid them over hers. She asked
again, every few minutes. Each time I gave her different answers
feeding them to her one by one like small grapes. She ate
them all. *You're lulling me…I feel like I'm in a forest, the leaves…*
She drifted off murmuring, then: *What nonsense!* She stared at
me as if I had tripped her. Later, she smiled when I said
goodbye, but before I could gather my things,
I was once more the stranger, unknown.

The last time the lines of her face had darkened, stilled. I slipped
in, hovered above her, placing one hand here, another there. Her eyes
unveiled into translucent green, watched me from inside of her
forest, the smell of wood softening, folding under her feet, wind
lifting the leaves, sending them whispering. She knew everything
there was to know.

Wood Smoke

We sit here, in
this minute considering
the next and the next
and the next as

though they were perfectly
placed paving stones walking
us with even steps
into the future.

Somewhere, though, up
ahead, their edges
soften and fold
eventually disappearing into

grass or earth,
swamp or trees. Still, on
the near horizon a gauzy
image hovers, sharpens

and reshapes. Here, in this
moment we sit
surrounded by our
inventions sensing

impossibility like the faint
trace of wood smoke in hair.
Yet already, the space
between the cells

has turned, found the
underside of what,
much later our eyes will
see as next.

What I Get from Reading Poetry

How to walk into the room of the indescribable, notice
    its furniture. How to walk back out of it,
look down and see that you now have
    a red tweed pillow in your arms.

Snowstorm

There is little to do and less
    to wonder about,
        like the snow that has now

stopped. The when of it
    has been replaced by quick glances
        out the window. There's no more

looking towards the bright
    cone below the streetlamp to see
        if it is empty or filled with flakes.

The power is holding,
    the road is open and for now,
        that's enough.

In the grocery store
    a crowd clumps around
        around the night-time medicines

and analgesics while large
    rubber doors marked No Exit
        whoomp in a slow uneven beat.

behind the cough and clatter.
    We back away and wander
        elsewhere. The aisles of

the store have gotten
    narrower, the shelves
        taller, stacked with canned

soups and sandwich cream
    cookies that loom beyond
        our reach. It's hard for our carts

to pass each other. Sometimes
        the grates catch and scrape
                on a wheel

will lock sideways, and someone
        has to back up and go
                around. Our house

is becoming like
        that too. The bookshelves
                have been made into pantries

while the books themselves
        are elsewhere, stacked in
                small towers next to instruments

we no longer
        play, leaving us
                to navigate the rooms

like giants in Legoland.
        Later, both of us now moving
                in and out of sickness, we wait,

wait for that one last
        round of fever to build
                and break. Afternoons

are the worst. The virtual world
        grows, lays draped like a large bubble
                across the crest of our snow-covered roof,

leans up against the chimney
and rumbles like a hungry
mammal. We reach for our

phones, tap them open
and slip inside. Stories of a fallen
cyber king and revived athletes loom

around us alongside
sales of snowflake face masks.
Hours pass in this way.

the silence deepens,
walks us back
to the window

and the view of the road.
A new layer of snow
has now almost buried the tracks.

The cars that do come
stop in front of our house
just short of the place where

the road slopes steeply downwards.
Mostly they back away, like some cats
do when you throw a red fuzzy ball

their way. It's a day like any
other. It's a day like nothing
we've ever seen.

With Gratitude

Deep gratitude and thanks to those who published some
of these poems and to those who did not but who took the
time to write the kind of encouraging words that helped me
to keep going in the work.

To Ann Pancake who insisted on seeing my work that I
had, until then, hardly let see the light of day and then for
convincing me that it was good.

To Jeanine Walker who not only taught me everything I
know about publishing but how to see and to grow the
work. To my cohort, Kathy, Seth and Paula who gave me the
beautiful, valuable and truthful feedback every writer craves.

To the Gerald Bigelow and Edmonds Poetry Group for their
support and for helping me to walk further out into the
world with the work.

And to the two people without whom I could not have
written anything whatsoever:
my deep friend Celia Smith who not only listened but who
always helps me find the words for all of the most important
things in life and to Shannon, my beloved.

Carol Tiebout lives in Edmonds, WA, on the traditional land of the Salish peoples where she is an active member of the local literary community. She began writing fiction during her time as a student at Western Washington State University. Her focus shifted to poetry in mid-life when she began working in hospice. Her poems can be found in *New Ohio Review, Calyx Journal of Art and Literature, BoomerLitMag* and *Neologism Poetry Journal.* Her poem "Water and Straw" won the first-place poetry prize in the Soul Making Keats literary competition.

www.ingramcontent.com/pod-product-compliance
Lightning Source LLC
Chambersburg PA
CBHW022101080426

42734CB00009B/1447